DOGS SET IX

AMERICAN PIT BULL TERRIERS

Joanne Mattern
ABDO Publishing Company

visit us at
www.abdopublishing.com

Published by ABDO Publishing Company, 8000 West 78th Street, Edina, Minnesota 55439. Copyright © 2012 by Abdo Consulting Group, Inc. International copyrights reserved in all countries. No part of this book may be reproduced in any form without written permission from the publisher. The Checkerboard Library™ is a trademark and logo of ABDO Publishing Company.

Printed in the United States of America, North Mankato, Minnesota.
062011
092011

Cover Photo: © Mark Raycroft / Kimball Stock
Interior Photos: Alamy pp. 7, 9, 15; Getty Images pp. 17, 21; Mark Raycroft / Minden Pictures / National Geographic Stock pp. 4, 11, 13, 19; Thinkstock p. 20

Editors: Megan M. Gunderson, BreAnn Rumsch
Art Direction: Neil Klinepier

Library of Congress Cataloging-in-Publication Data

Mattern, Joanne, 1963-
  American pit bull terriers / Joanne Mattern.
     p. cm. -- (Dogs)
  Includes index.
  ISBN 978-1-61714-988-7
  1. American pit bull terrier--Juvenile literature. I. Title.
  SF429.A72M37 2012
  636.755'9--dc22
                          2011009394

CONTENTS

THE DOG FAMILY

Dogs are one of the most popular pets in the world. Americans alone own more than 75 million dogs!

Before you adopt an American pit bull terrier, do your research. Some communities do not allow people to own this breed.

There are more than 400 dog **breeds** to choose from. Amazingly, all those different breeds belong to the family **Canidae**. This name comes from the Latin word *canis*, which means "dog." Scientists believe all dogs originally descended from the gray wolf.

People and dogs have been companions for more than 12,000 years. During this time, dogs have helped humans with hunting, herding, and guarding.

In addition to these important jobs, some dogs have been raised for fighting. Today, dogfighting is illegal in the United States and Canada. The practice is considered cruel, but it does still occur.

One dog breed that was often raised to be **aggressive** toward other dogs is the American pit bull terrier. However, many people believe these dogs do not deserve their bad reputation. With the right care and training, American pit bull terriers can make great family pets.

AMERICAN PIT BULL TERRIERS

American pit bull terriers come from bulldog and terrier ancestors. These dogs were originally **bred** in England to be good fighters. They were supposed to be **aggressive** toward other dogs, but not toward humans.

In the 1800s, **immigrants** brought these loyal dogs to the United States. There, they eventually became known as American pit bull terriers.

The breed remained popular for dogfighting. Yet not all of these dogs were bred to fight. Some drove cattle for ranchers. Others hauled carts for miners. And, many American pit bull terriers became treasured family pets.

These intelligent dogs are eager to please and make devoted pets for many owners.

The **United Kennel Club (UKC)** has recognized the American pit bull terrier since 1898. The **American Kennel Club** does not recognize this **breed**.

What They're Like

American pit bull terriers are strong, confident dogs. They should not act shy or timid. These dogs like to be where the action is! They love to have fun, and they often act silly and goofy.

This **breed** tends to be friendly around children and adults. However, American pit bull terriers do not always get along well with other dogs. They may show **aggression** when first meeting other dogs. Yet some can be trained to get along with other family pets.

American pit bull terriers have lots of energy! They like to play and need daily walks. Giving them plenty of toys to play with is the best way to keep American

pit bull terriers out of trouble. Good training is also important. These powerful dogs must know how to follow directions and behave.

American pit bull terriers are often so friendly they do not make good watchdogs!

Coat and Color

American pit bull terriers have almost every coat color and pattern except **merle**. They may display a mix of colors. Often, their coats are white mixed with another color.

The American pit bull terrier has a short, smooth coat. The coat does not tangle or get **matted**, so it is easy to care for. It **sheds** lightly year-round. In spring and fall, it sheds more.

This dog **breed** is easy to groom. American pit bull terriers only need weekly brushing. They should be bathed about every eight weeks unless they get really dirty!

A glossy coat means
a healthy dog!

SIZE

Most American pit bull terriers are medium-sized dogs, but some are larger. Males should weigh between 35 and 60 pounds (16 and 27 kg). Females are a little smaller. They should weigh 30 to 50 pounds (14 to 23 kg). On average, this **breed** is 18 to 22 inches (46 to 56 cm) tall.

American pit bull terriers often have a square shape. These dogs are just about as tall as they are long. This gives these strong, athletic dogs their powerful look. The breed's thick muscles also add to its stocky, square appearance. But, these dogs should not be too bulky.

The American pit bull terrier is an expressive dog. Its wide-set eyes are medium sized. The **UKC** allows any eye color except blue. The **breed** has a wide **muzzle** and a large nose. Its chest is deep and its medium-length tail tapers to a point. Its ears are small to medium and set high on the head.

When an American pit bull terrier is concentrating, wrinkles form on its forehead.

CARE

Caring for American pit bull terriers is a great way for owners to bond with their pets. These dogs can have sensitive skin, so take care when brushing or bathing them.

Carefully clean their ears with a soft, damp cloth. And, brush their teeth at least a few times a week. Be sure to use a dog toothpaste and not your own!

It is also important to keep a dog's nails short. Walking on sidewalks or pavement will naturally wear down the dog's nails. But if you hear your dog's nails clicking on the floor, it's time for a trim! Use a special nail clipper or grinding tool. Untrimmed nails can lead to damaged or sore paws.

American pit bull terriers are generally healthy dogs.

Regular checkups with a veterinarian are a must for any dog. This doctor will make sure American pit bull terriers are healthy and give them **vaccines**. He or she will also **spay** or **neuter** dogs when they are about six months old.

FEEDING

All dogs need high-quality food to stay healthy and strong. Dog food can be dry, wet, or semimoist. American pit bull terriers should be fed at the same time every day. Puppies start out eating four to five times a day. Adults usually eat two meals daily.

Your dog's diet will depend on its age and activity level. Too much food and not enough exercise can lead to an overweight dog. So be sure not to overfeed your American pit bull terrier. Don't feed it table scraps, as these can be unhealthy. And, don't leave food out all day for your dog to graze on.

Water is another key part of an American pit bull terrier's diet. So, have a clean bowl of fresh water available all day. This will help keep your dog healthy.

American pit bull terriers can suffer from a serious stomach problem called bloat. To prevent this, don't let your dog eat or drink too much too quickly.

THINGS THEY NEED

American pit bull terriers are active dogs. These fun-loving pets enjoy taking walks with their owners. Using a leash will help keep American pit bull terriers safe on walks. Every dog should also have a collar with license and identification tags. This helps people return lost dogs to their owners.

Keeping dogs active and providing a variety of toys will help keep them out of trouble. It will also help prevent excessive barking. And, chew toys will save your things from puppy teeth!

Dogs are required to have licenses almost everywhere in the United States. To be licensed, dogs must have up-to-date vaccines.

Before anyone brings home a new pet, they need to get ready! New owners should have food and water bowls for the dog. A crate is a good place for a dog to sleep. It should be lined with a pad or a blanket. A soft bed is another good choice.

PUPPIES

Female American pit bull terriers are **pregnant** for about 63 days. Medium-sized dogs usually give birth to **litters** of four to eight puppies. Puppies can't see or hear for one to two weeks. They need to stay with their mother until they are at least eight to twelve weeks old.

Dog lovers can find American pit bull terrier puppies from knowledgeable **breeders**. This breed is often available from rescue groups or animal shelters, too. However, it is important to learn as much as possible about a dog before adopting it.

American pit bull terrier puppies should be **socialized** from a young age. Owners need to introduce their puppies to different animals, people, and places. They should also train puppies to follow commands. Healthy American pit bull terriers will keep their owners company for 10 to 12 years.

These intelligent dogs have good memories. If you let your little puppy up on the couch, it will expect to keep doing this as a big dog!

GLOSSARY

aggressive (uh-GREH-sihv) - displaying hostility.

American Kennel Club - an organization that studies and promotes interest in purebred dogs.

breed - a group of animals sharing the same ancestors and appearance. A breeder is a person who raises animals. Raising animals is often called breeding them.

Canidae (KAN-uh-dee) - the scientific Latin name for the dog family. Members of this family are called canids. They include wolves, jackals, foxes, coyotes, and domestic dogs.

immigrant - a person who enters another country to live.

litter - all of the puppies born at one time to a mother dog.

matted - forming a tangled mass.

merle - having dark patches of color on a lighter background.

muzzle - an animal's nose and jaws.

neuter (NOO-tuhr) - to remove a male animal's reproductive glands.

pregnant - having one or more babies growing within the body.

shed - to cast off hair, feathers, skin, or other coverings or parts by a natural process.

socialize - to accustom an animal or a person to spending time with others.

spay - to remove a female animal's reproductive organs.

United Kennel Club (UKC) - an organization that registers purebred dogs and promotes events that test their skills.

vaccine (vak-SEEN) - a shot given to prevent illness or disease.

WEB SITES

To learn more about American pit bull terriers, visit ABDO Publishing Company online. Web sites about American pit bull terriers are featured on our Book Links page. These links are routinely monitored and updated to provide the most current information available.

www.abdopublishing.com

INDEX